D1093258

Shrimp
Science Under The Sea

Lynn M. Stone

Rourke
Publishing LLC
Vero Beach, Florida 32964

PHOTO CREDITS: Cover, title page, p. 4, 7, 12, 15 © James H. Carmichael; p. 8,
10, 13 © Brandon Cole; p. 16, 20 © Marty Snyderman; p. 19 © Lynn M. Stone.

Cover Photo: *The hingebeak shrimp of Indonesia*

EDITOR: Frank Sloan

COVER DESIGN: Nicola Stratford

Library of Congress Cataloging-in-Publication Data

Stone, Lynn M.
  Shrimp / Lynn M. Stone.
     p. cm. — (Science under the sea)
Summary: Describes the physical characteristics, behavior, habitat, and
life cycle of shrimp.
Includes bibliographical references (p.   ).
  ISBN 1-58952-321-0 (hardcover)
  1. Shrimps—Juvenile literature. [1. Shrimps.] I. Title.
  QL444.M33 S68 2002
  595.3'88—dc21
                                                    2002005132

Printed in the USA

CG/CG

Table of Contents

Small, Boneless Animals

Shrimp are often called shellfish, along with crabs, lobsters, clams, and oysters. In fact, none of these animals is a fish.

Shrimp and their crab and lobster cousins belong to a group of small, boneless animals called **crustaceans**. Crayfish, or crawdads, are also crustaceans.

Like their lobster and crab cousins, shrimp arc protected by a shell.

Living in Shells

Like other crustaceans, shrimp live in shells. Although it's outside the shrimp's body, the shell is the shrimp's skeleton. The shell supports and protects the shrimp's soft body.

A solid shell wouldn't allow a shrimp, or any crustacean, to bend. But shrimp and other crustacean shells are built in **segments**, or sections. There is a joint where segments meet. The joints allow the shrimp to bend.

A banded coral shrimp bends at its shell joints while eating a smaller shrimp.

Many Kinds and Sizes

There are several hundred kinds of shrimp. Some kinds live only in salt water. Others live only in fresh water.

Shrimp are often finger-sized animals. The smallest shrimp are less than 1 inch (fewer than 2.2 centimeters) long. The largest kinds of shrimp grow more than 1 foot (.30 meters) long. These "big" shrimp live in fresh water.

The tiny clown shrimp lives in the company of a sea anemone, whose stinging tentacles protect it from fish.

Shrimp Bodies

Shrimp come in many colors, including gray, white, brown, and pink. Peppermint shrimp wear bright stripes. Some kinds of shrimp can change their color. In that way they can blend in with their surroundings.

A shrimp's body has three main sections: head, **thorax**, and **abdomen**. The head and thorax fit together under a single segment of shell.

One of the most colorful shrimp, a hingebeak crawls down a sponge.

A transparent cleaner shrimp hides among the tentacles of a sea anemone.

Coleman's shrimp are safe from fish predators when they stay among the poisonous spines of a sea urchin.

Shrimp Appendages

From each body segment of a shrimp, several long, sharp body parts reach out. The parts do different things for a shrimp. Together, however, they are called **appendages**.

A shrimp's many appendages give it a spiky look and feel. Appendages are evenly set. Most shrimp have 19 pairs of appendages. They include two pair of whip-like **antennae**, or feelers, on the shrimp's head. They also include jointed legs and flattened appendages used for swimming and carrying eggs.

Long appendages on shrimp give them a spiky look and feel.

Growing a New Shell

As a shrimp grows, it becomes too big for its shell. The shell cracks and the shrimp slips out. While the shrimp hides, its body produces a new, larger shell.

The mantis shrimp is armed with powerful claws as well as a shell.

Predator and Prey

If you have a taste for shrimp, you're not alone. Shrimp are important **prey** for many **predators**, such as fish and birds.

Some shrimp are predators, too. Many shrimp hunt at night. With their mouthparts and little, plier-like claws called **pincers**, they catch small marine animals.

A white ibis grabs a shrimp from the surf.

Snappers and Cleaners

Shrimp do many unusual things. For example, certain kinds of shrimp begin their lives as males. When they are about two years old, they become females.

Cleaning shrimp have a curious relationship with fish. Certain kinds of fish let the cleaning shrimp pick dead skin and unwanted little critters off their bodies. Both the shrimp and fish gain from the arrangement.

A black-spotted toadfish is cleaned by a cleaner shrimp in the South Pacific Ocean.

Snapping shrimp make gunshot noises. Their pincers are very large. When snapped shut they are loud enough to stun small fish. That makes the fish easy for the shrimp to catch. Scientists believe the snapping noise has other purposes, too. It may help shrimp communicate with each other.

Glossary

abdomen (AB doh mun) — the last section of a crustacean's body after the head and thorax

antennae (ann TEN ee) — feelers

appendages (ah PEN daj ez) — separate smaller body parts attached to the main body

crustaceans (crus TAY shunz) — a large group of related, boneless animals whose bodies are in sections and are covered by a shell

pincers (PIN surz) — little claws that grasp like pliers

predators (PRED eh torz) — animals that hunt other animals for food

prey (PRAY) — an animal hunted by other animals

segments (SEG muntz) — sections of shell or body that form part of the whole

thorax (THOR acks) — the section of a crustacean's body between its head and abdomen

1375460

Index

Further Reading

Chanko, Pamela. *Sea Creatures*. Scholastic, 1998
Meucci, Antonella. *Seas and Oceans*. Gareth Stevens, 2000
Ricciuti, Edward R. *Crustaceans*. Gale Group, 1993

Websites To Visit

Crustaceans: http://www.seasky.org/reeflife/sea2e.html
Crabs and Shrimp: http://www.seasky.org/links/sealink02.html

About The Author

Lynn Stone is the author of more than 400 children's nonfiction books. He is a talented natural history photographer as well. Lynn, a former teacher, travels worldwide to photograph wildlife in its natural habitat.